PAPER GIFTS

Jennifer Sanderson and
Jessica Moon

ARCTURUS

This edition first published in 2015 by Arcturus Publishing

Distributed by Black Rabbit Books
P.O. Box 3263
Mankato
Minnesota MN 56002

Models and photography: Jessica Moon
Text: Jennifer Sanderson
Editors: Becca Clunes and Joe Harris
Designer: Jessica Moon

Library of Congress Cataloging-in-Publication Data

Sanderson, Jennifer, author.
 Paper gifts / Jennifer Sanderson & Jessica Moon.
    pages cm. -- (Origami and papercraft)
 Audience: Grades 4 to 6.
 Includes bibliographical references and index.
 ISBN 978-1-78404-085-7
 1. Origami--Juvenile literature. 2. Paper work--Juvenile literature. I. Moon, Jessica, designer. II. Title.
 TT872.5.S2637 2015
 736.982--dc23
                          2013048243

Printed in China

SL004079US
Supplier 29, Date 0514, Print Run 3407

Contents

Introduction...4

Treat Holder..8

Bookmark...10

Envelope..14

Tulip..16

Coaster...22

Gift Box...27

Glossary..32

Further Reading...32

Web Sites...32

Index...32

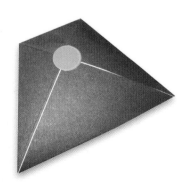

Introduction

Origami has been popular in Japan for hundreds of years and is now loved all around the world. You can make great models with just one sheet of paper and this book shows you how!

The paper used in origami is thin but strong, so that it can be folded many times. It is usually colored on one side. Alternatively, you can use ordinary scrap paper but make sure it's not too thick.

Origami models often share the same folds and basic designs, known as "bases." This introduction explains some of the folds and bases that you will need for the projects in this book. When making the models, follow the key below to find out what the lines and arrows mean. Always crease your paper well!

MOUNTAIN FOLD

To make a mountain fold, fold the paper so that the crease is pointing up toward you, like a mountain.

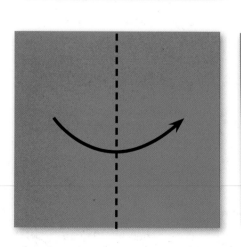

VALLEY FOLD

To make a valley fold, fold the paper the other way, so that the crease is pointing away from you, like a valley.

INSIDE REVERSE FOLD

An inside reverse fold is useful if you want to flatten the shape of part of your model.

1 Practice by first folding a piece of paper diagonally in half. Make a valley fold on one point and crease.

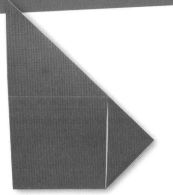

2 It's important to make sure that the paper is creased well. Run your finger over the crease two or three times.

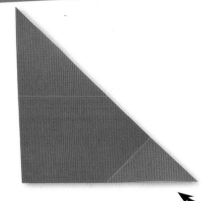

Open

3 Unfold and open up the corner slightly. Refold the crease nearest to you into a mountain fold.

4 Open up the paper a little more and then tuck the tip of the point inside. This is the view from the underside of the paper. Close the paper.

5 Flatten the paper. You now have an inside reverse fold.

KEY

valley fold — – – – – – – – – – – – – – – – – –

mountain fold — •••••••••••••••••••••••••

step fold (mountain and valley fold next to each other)

direction to move paper ⟶

direction to push or pull ◄

5

WATERBOMB BASE

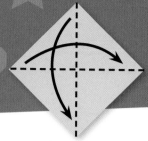

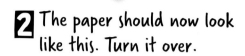

1 Start with a square of paper, with the point toward you. Make two diagonal valley folds.

2 The paper should now look like this. Turn it over.

3 Make two valley folds along the horizontal and vertical lines.

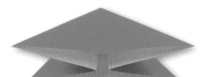

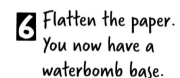

4 Push the paper into this shape, so the center spot pops up.

5 Push in the sides, so that the back and front sections are brought together.

6 Flatten the paper. You now have a waterbomb base.

KITE BASE

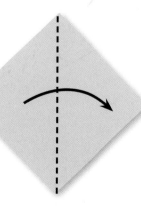

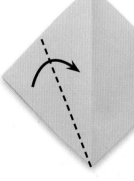

1 Start with the point turned toward you. Valley fold it in half diagonally and then unfold.

2 Valley fold the left section to meet the center crease.

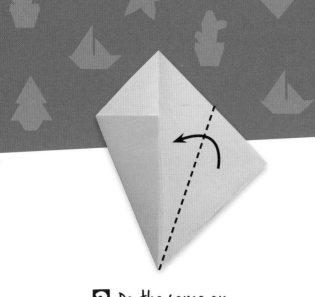

3 Do the same on the other side.

4 You now have a kite base.

BLINTZ BASE

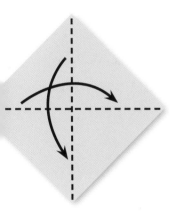

1 Start with a square of paper, with the point toward you. Make two diagonal valley folds.

2 The paper should now look like this. Fold the bottom point up to the center.

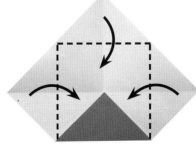

3 Repeat step 2 with the three remaining points.

4 You now have a blintz base.

Treat Holder

This little pouch is a perfect way to give someone candies or chocolates. You could decorate the treat holder with hearts if it's for Valentine's day or balloons for a birthday gift.

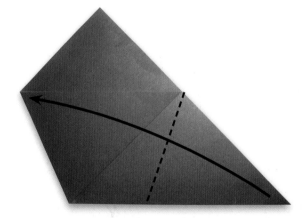

Yummy!

START WITH YOUR PAPER COLORED SIDE DOWN

1 Valley fold your paper in half from bottom to top.

2 Valley fold the top triangle down so that the left side meets the bottom. Crease well and then unfold.

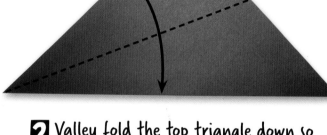

3 Valley fold the bottom-left point over to the right so that it meets the far end of the previous fold.

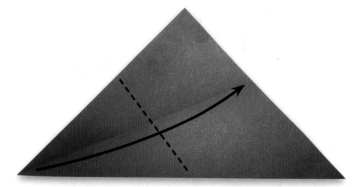

4 Valley fold the bottom-right point over to the left to meet the left point.

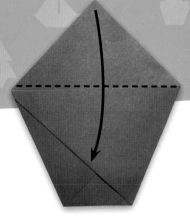

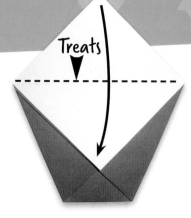

Treats

5 Valley fold the top flap of the triangle down to create your pocket.

6 Your model should look like this. Decorate the model if you like then place your treats inside the pocket. Fold the top triangle down to close it.

7

Use a special sticker or stamp to seal your treat box before you give it away.

Bookmark

If you know someone who loves to read, you could make them this clever origami bookmark. What a fun way to mark the pages of your favorite book!

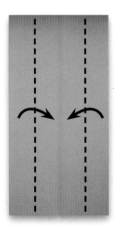

So cute!

START WITH YOUR PAPER COLORED SIDE UP

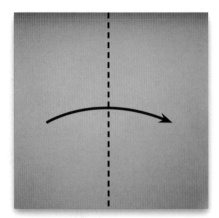

1 Valley fold your paper in half from left to right. Crease and then unfold.

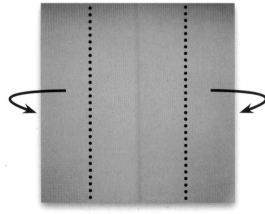

2 Mountain fold the left and right sides in half to create a rectangle.

3 Valley fold the left and right sides in half. Crease well and then unfold.

4 Valley fold the top left corner to meet the first left fold, crease, and then unfold.

5 Using the bottom point of the corner fold of step 4 as a guide, mountain fold the top of the paper behind your rectangle and crease well.

6 Valley fold the top left and right corners into the center.

7 Mountain fold the top triangle to create a straight top.

8 Valley fold the right side in half and at the same time lift the top right section up. Flatten the top section.

9 Your paper should now look like this. Repeat step 8 on the left side.

DID YOU KNOW?
Bookmarks first appeared in the medieval period. Early books were very expensive to make, so something was needed to mark a reader's place without causing damage.

10 Valley fold each of the top four corners.

Close-up of top folds.

11 Valley fold the bottom two corners to shape the bottom of your bookmark.

12 Your model should look like this. Turn your model over.

13 Your bookmark is ready. Why not make this bookmark to go with a book as a gift?

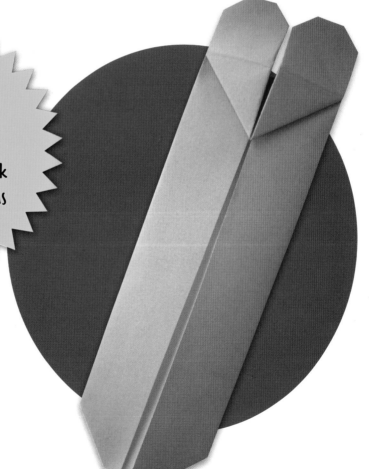

Envelope

This elegant envelope will look amazing with a personalized greetings card or a handwritten letter inside it.

START WITH YOUR PAPER COLORED SIDE DOWN

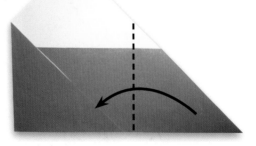

Clever!

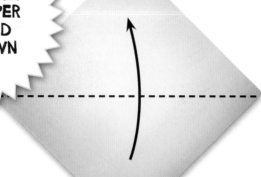

1 Valley fold your paper in half from bottom to top.

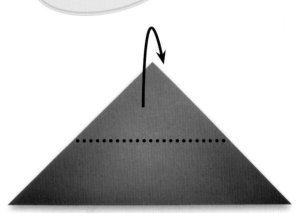

2 Mountain fold the top flap in half horizontally and tuck it behind itself.

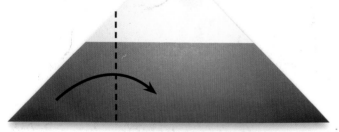

3 Valley fold the left point over to the right.

4 Valley fold the right point over to the left side. Make sure this fold is the same size as the fold from step 3.

Medium

5 Valley fold the top flap over to the right where it crosses the bottom flap.

Lift

6 Lift up the triangle you have just created so that it points toward you.

Press

7 Press the triangle point down to flatten it into a diamond.

8 Valley fold the top point down and tuck it into the little square flap to close the envelope.

9 Carefully open the envelope and place a card or letter inside it, closing it when you've finished.

Merry Christmas!

Tulip

This tulip may be tricky to make, but it is really pretty and makes a lovely gift to give to your mom or a friend.

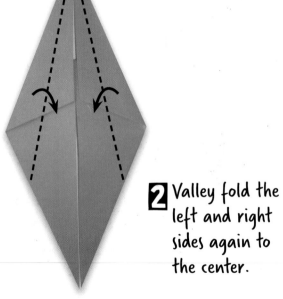

START WITH A KITE BASE

Pretty!

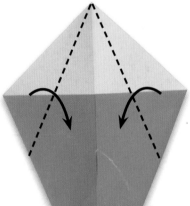

1 To make the stem and leaf, choose green paper. Valley fold the left and right sides to the center.

2 Valley fold the left and right sides again to the center.

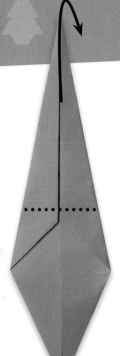

3 Mountain fold
your model in
half horizontally.

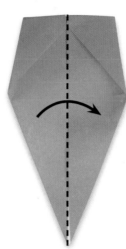

4 Valley fold the left side
over to the right, crease
well, and then unfold.

5 Unfold the mountain
fold from step 3.
Turn your model over
so it looks like the
picture in step 6.

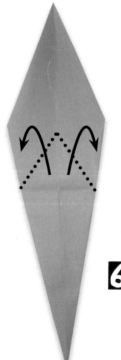

6 Mountain fold the top
sides of your paper to
shape a leaf for your
stem. Use your fingers
to crease the paper and
give shape to your leaf.

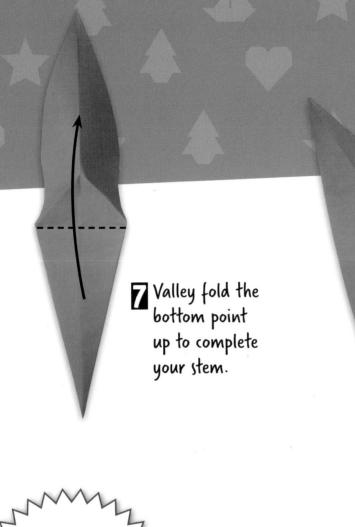

7 Valley fold the bottom point up to complete your stem.

8 Your model should now stand up. Put it to one side while you make your flower.

START
WITH A
WATERBOMB
BASE

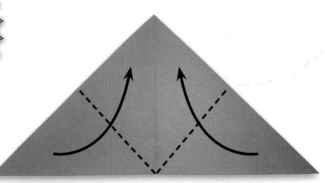

9 To make the petals, choose a color such as pink, red, or yellow. Place your waterbomb base with the point at the top. Valley fold the top left and right points up into the center.

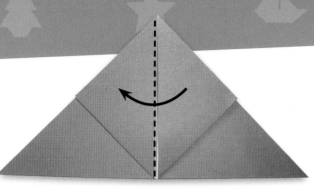

10 Valley fold the top right flap over to the left.

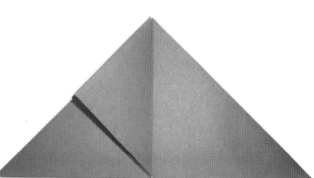

11 Your paper should now look like this. Turn it over and repeat steps 9 and 10 on the reverse:

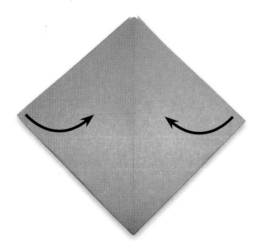

12 Take the top left and right flaps and slot the right flap into the pocket of the left flap as far as you can.

Close-up of flaps.

Press   Press

13 Your model should look like this. Carefully press down to flatten the paper, making sure the sides are equal.

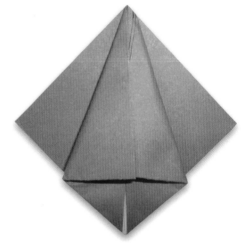

14 Your model should look like this. Turn it over and repeat steps 12 and 13 on the reverse.

DID YOU KNOW?
The name "tulip" comes from the Persian word for "turban"—probably because of the flower's shape!

Hold here

Blow here

15 Your model should look like this. Blow gently into the bottom end to inflate your tulip.

16 Your model should now look like this. Gently pull back the top layers to create petals.

17 Your model should now look like this.

18 To finish your tulip, carefully place your flower on the finished stem from step 8. Isn't it pretty?

Coaster

This flower coaster is an attractive way to make sure your glass or cup doesn't leave a mark on the table.

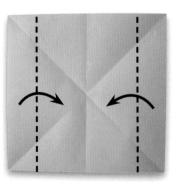

Great!

START WITH YOUR PAPER COLORED SIDE DOWN

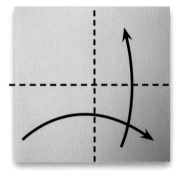

1 Valley fold your paper in half from the bottom to top and from left to right. Unfold it.

2 Valley fold your paper in half diagonally as shown. Crease well and unfold.

3 Valley fold the left and right sides so that they meet in the center.

4 Valley fold the top and bottom edges up into the center, crease well, and then unfold.

5 Valley fold the top left and right flaps out to the sides.

Pull

6 Your model should look like this. Pull the top flap down so that it lies flat.

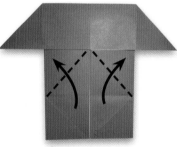

7 Repeat steps 5 and 6 on the bottom half.

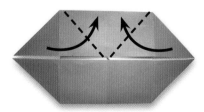

8 Valley fold the top left and right sides up.

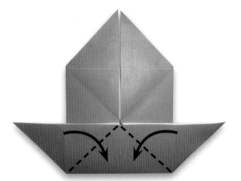

9 Valley fold the bottom left and right sides down.

10 Valley fold the top left triangle so that the top is pointing toward you.

11 Your model should now look like this. Now, open up the flap.

12 Press the corner down to flatten.

13 Your model should look like this. Repeat steps 10, 11, and 12 on the three remaining triangles.

14 Valley fold the corners of the top-left square into the center of the square.

15 Your model should look like this. Repeat step 14 on the three remaining squares.

open

16 Your model should look like this. Now, open the top left flaps.

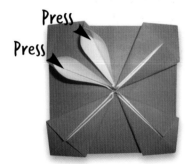

Press

Press

17 Press the open flaps down to flatten them.

18 Your model should look like this. Repeat steps 16 and 17 on the three remaining squares.

19 Your coaster should look like this.

20 You can rest your glass or cup on your finished coaster. You could make a set of four as a gift for someone.

Gift Box

Fill this pretty little gift box with candy or other treats to make a lovely present.

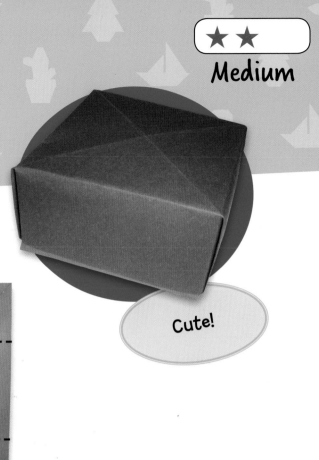

Cute!

START WITH A BLINTZ BASE

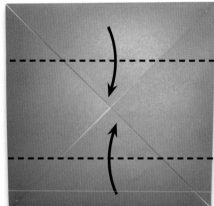

1 Valley fold the top and bottom sides into the center, crease well, and then unfold.

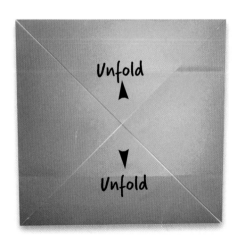

Unfold

Unfold

2 Unfold the top and bottom triangles.

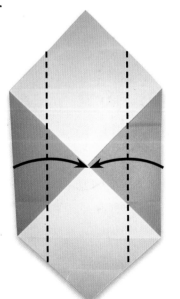

3 Valley fold the left and right sides into the center.

4 Valley fold the top and bottom diagonally, crease well, and then unfold.

5 Valley fold the top and bottom diagonally again, but in the other direction, crease well, and then unfold.

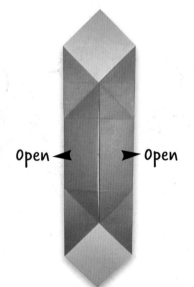

Open ◄ ► Open

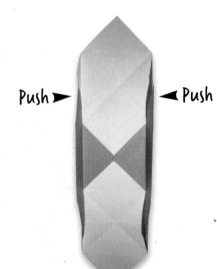

Push ► ◄ Push

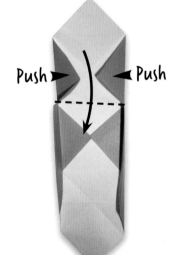

Push ► ◄ Push

6 Now open the left and right flaps so that they are pointing upward.

7 Your model should look like this. Push in the top of the sides to collapse them.

8 Valley fold the top while pushing in the sides to form another side of your box.

9 Valley fold the top to complete the side and bottom. Use your fingers to flatten the top to the side and bottom.

10 Your model should now look like this. Repeat steps 7, 8, and 9 on the remaining side.

11 Your box should now look like this. To create a lid, use a slightly bigger piece of paper and repeat steps 1 to 10.

12 Fill your box with treats. Add the bow on page 30 to make it even more special.

Gift Bow

Attach this striking bow to any present to add a personal, stylish touch!

Stylish!

START WITH A BLINTZ BASE

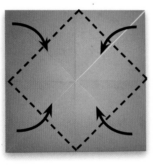

1 To make the bow, place your blintz base so that the flaps are facing up. Fold the points into the center.

2 Your model should look like this. Turn your model over.

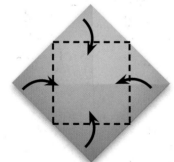

3 Fold the points into the center, as you would to make a blintz base.

4 Valley fold the flaps out, so that they overlap the edges.

5 Your model should look like this. Turn your model over.

30

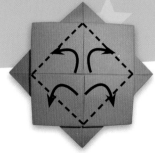

6 Valley fold and lift the top flaps so that they point upward.

7 Valley fold and lift the bottom flaps so that they point upward.

Happy Birthday!

8 Your gift bow is ready. You can write a greeting inside for a personal touch.

9 Why not use your bow to decorate your gift box from page 27?

Glossary

base A simple, folded shape that is used as the starting point for many different origami projects.

blintz base An origami shape named after a thin pancake and formed by folding all four corners of a paper square to the center point.

crease A line in a piece of paper made by folding.

mountain fold An origami step where a piece of paper is folded so that the crease is pointing upward, like a mountain.

step fold A mountain fold and a valley fold next to each other.

valley fold An origami step where a piece of paper is folded so that the crease is pointing downward, like a valley.

Further Reading

My First Origami Book by Susan Akass (CICO Kidz, 2011)
Origami for Children by Mari Ono (CICO Books, 2009)
Origami Kit for Dummies by Nick Robinson (John Wiley & Sons, 2008)
World's Best Origami by Nick Robinson (Alpha Books, 2010)

Web Sites

http://www.origami-make.com A wide-ranging origami page, featuring instructions for making a variety of paper gifts—from butterflies to boxes and sweets to shoes!
http://www.origamidatabase.com/ An origami database containing instructions for hundreds of paper projects.

Index

B
blintz bases 7, 27, 30
bookmarks 10–13

C
coasters 22–26

E
envelopes 14–15

G
gift bows 30–31
gift boxes 27–29

K
kite bases 6, 16

P
petals 18–21

S
stems 16–18, 21

T
treat holders 8–9
tulips 16–21

W
waterbomb bases 6, 18